When we need the ultimate
in compassion —
the greatest caring, true concern —
it is God's love that wipes each tear away
and brings tomorrow's hope

God isn't far away...
He's always by your side

— Barbara J. Hall

Blue Mountain Arts ®
Bestselling Titles

By Susan Polis Schutz:

To My Daughter, with Love, on the Important Things in Life

To My Son, with Love

I Love You

By Douglas Pagels:

For You, Just Because You're Very Special to Me

May You Always Have an Angel by Your Side

To the One Person I Consider to Be My Soul Mate

Is It Time to Make a Change?
by Deanna Beisser

To the Love of My Life
by Donna Fargo

Anthologies:

Always Believe in Yourself and Your Dreams

For You, My Daughter

Friends for Life

I Love You, Mom

I'm Glad You Are My Sister

The Joys and Challenges of Motherhood

The Language of Recovery

Marriage Is a Promise of Love

Teaching and Learning Are Lifelong Journeys

There Is Greatness Within You, My Son

Think Positive Thoughts Every Day

Thoughts to Share with a Wonderful Teenager

With God by Your Side ...You Never Have to Be Alone

GOD
Is Always Watching Over You

An Inspirational Reminder
of God's Constant Presence
in Our Lives

A Blue Mountain Arts® Collection
Edited by Gary Morris

Blue Mountain Press™
Boulder, Colorado

Copyright © 2002, 2005 by Blue Mountain Arts, Inc.

Library of Congress Control Number: 2002094312
ISBN: 0-88396-924-6 (trade paper) — ISBN: 0-88396-675-1 (hardcover)

ACKNOWLEDGMENTS appear on page 64.

Certain trademarks are used under license.
BLUE MOUNTAIN PRESS is registered in U.S. Patent and Trademark Office.

Printed in the United States of America.
First printing of this edition: 2005

 This book is printed on recycled paper.

This book is printed on fine quality, laid embossed, 80 lb. paper. This paper has been specially produced to be acid free (neutral pH) and contains no groundwood or unbleached pulp. It conforms with all the requirements of the American National Standards Institute, Inc., so as to ensure that this book will last and be enjoyed by future generations.

Blue Mountain Arts, Inc.
P.O. Box 4549, Boulder, Colorado 80306

Contents

God Is Always Watching Over You

Someone's watching over you
    with the greatest love.
Someone wants you to be
    happy, safe, and secure.
Someone considers you
    a wonderful individual
    and cares about your needs.
Someone's making blessings
    for your benefit right now —
like sunshine for those rainy days
and rainbows to remind you
    of the promise up ahead.

Someone's watching over you always...
    and He will take good care of you.

— Barbara J. Hall

In God, You Will Find Everything You Need

God has all the strength you need.
It's a matter of letting go
and realizing you can't do it alone.
Whether or not you've prayed before
or have ever tried to trust Him,
now is the time to give Him a chance.

Life is a lot easier with God by your side,
not because things will always go your way
or nothing will ever go wrong again,
but because God gives you the strength
you need for every situation.

God loves you without conditions.
His love doesn't depend on anything;
it is a free gift from Him to you.

He helps you face temptation
and gives you what it takes to walk away.
He can be your shield against a harsh world,
your rainbows to believe in through the storms,
and your answer to every problem.

The important thing to remember
is that you are never alone
because you always have God...
and He is always enough.

— Barbara Cage

God Will Carry You Through to New Dreams and Hopes

In the shelter of God's love,
there is comfort
for all of life's ups and downs.
In the hollow of His heart,
there's a place only you can fill.
In God's time, you will find new dreams,
new growth taking place.
In waiting for Him to come,
you'll find He's already here.
In every dream and every dawn,
touch the prayers urging you
to keep trying.
In every concern,
feel the caring belief for a better day.
In every trial, there are lessons
your heart can learn.

May God give each day new meaning
and time give each dream new wings.
May God scatter your cares to the wind
as He carries you close to His heart.

— Linda E. Knight

Have Faith!

When you dream, believe
in your ability to fulfill your wishes.
Believe — have faith —
and you will exceed your own expectations.

When you work, treat each task as a gift
and a chance to demonstrate your strengths.
Believe — have faith —
and each duty will bring a sense of purpose.

When you regret some past mistake or failure,
don't allow pessimism to influence you.
Believe — have faith —
and know that your past is gone.
Tomorrow you'll have a second chance to atone.

When you hurt and no one seems to understand,
reach into your heart and be your own comfort.
You have the strength within.
Believe — have faith —
and your pain will pass into yesterday.

When you love, love with all your heart and soul.
Give without limit or expectation.
Believe — have faith —
and love will inspire your entire life.

Believe — have faith —
and remember that you are God's child...
and whatever He designs is perfect.

— Regina Hill

There's an Angel on Your Shoulder

Have you ever felt that inner tug
  or a silent voice of caution
    or an invisible hand
      leading you down some new path?
Has the light of an exciting new idea
  suddenly lit up in your mind,
    or has an inner sense of love made you
      rise up to help someone in need?
If you look closely
  you might just see
    an angel sitting on your shoulder!
This heavenly messenger is your own
  personal guardian sent to keep you
    safe and lead you down the steep
      paths of life.
Your angel will direct your steps
  and watch over you.
Don't worry. Don't give up.
  Just turn your head,
    and you will see your newest friend
      sitting on your shoulder...
  making sure everything is okay!

— Dan Lynch

You Can Lean on Prayer
for Strength and Support

Prayer is a way that our hearts
can communicate in faith,
A way that we can ask questions
and receive answers,
A way that we can openly express
our feelings and concerns.
Prayer is a wonderful source of
strength for a person,
And prayers can become even
stronger when we turn to each
other for support in prayer.
Lean on prayer to help you through
difficult times,
And know with certainty what the
power of prayer can do —
Especially when we pray together
for strength.

— Susan Hickman Sater

A Special Prayer for You

May God be with you
and bring you sweet peace.
May He fill your heart with cheer.
May He fill your voice with song.
May He quiet all your fears.

May God touch your life
    with kind hearts
    reaching out to you.
May His angels guide you.
May He remind you
    how much you mean to others.
May God keep you strong
    and believing
you have a friend in Him.

— Jacqueline Schiff

Some of the best advice
a person can share
	with someone they care about
		is this...

"God will be there for you."

If you need to lean on someone,
	there is no greater strength.
If you need to move away from
	difficulty and toward resolve,
		there is no greater direction to go.
If you wish to walk with happiness,
	there is no greater traveling companion.

	Follow your heart when it tells you
	to believe, because there is no end
		to the blessings
			you can receive.

		"God will be there
			for you."

						— Alin Austin

Face Your Challenges
with Victory in Mind

One of the hardest lessons to learn in life is
that there is no victory without a challenge...
and challenges only arise as we come face
to face with problems.

We will do anything to avoid problems. We ignore
them. We put them off. We pass them on to
someone else. We rationalize them away...
if we can.

But there is a spiritual strength that is developed
in the process of overcoming problems, and
it is in the overcoming that our lives take on
a firm foundation and a depth of character.

Problems that seem so overwhelming and
   beyond our human ability often serve
   to deepen our trust and faith that
   God will see us through — and, in the
   process, they draw us closer to Him.
It is so important to view a problem as
   a test of faith that will challenge our
   character until we overcome it... and
   we are victorious!
Take the challenge! And remember... the
   bigger the problem, the bigger
   the victory.

— Dan Lynch

Let God Help

He has helped so many through
   so much.
And He will be there for you
   in your most personal moments
   and through all the times of your life,
   whether they are troubled
   or triumphant.

Take comfort in that thought.
Hold it inside you
   this day and all the days
   of your life.

— Alin Austin

May These Blessings Be with You

THE BLESSING OF LOVE

May you love and be loved by the
people who mean the most to you.
May the love in your heart give you
a constant sense of balance, support,
and soulful and spiritual nourishment.

THE BLESSING OF HEALTH

May you have a healthy body, mind,
and spirit all the days of your life,
and may you deal successfully with
any health issues that occur.

THE BLESSING OF A JOYFUL HEART

May your attitude about life assist
you in loving others, as well as
yourself. May it help you to deal with
whatever you encounter in life: success,
failure, pleasure, disappointment, and
all the in-betweens.

THE BLESSING OF FAMILY
May you have a supportive family...
people to go home to... people
close to you who know where you
came from and where you are now...
people who care about where you
want to go from here.

THE BLESSING OF FRIENDSHIP
May you have friends who enrich
your life, care about you, and show
you that they care.

THE BLESSING OF HAPPINESS
May you always have a sense of
peace, contentment, and satisfaction
in your life. May you tap into this
source as you need encouragement
and hope and help, and may it guide
you on the pathways of your dreams.

— Donna Fargo

What God Hath Promised

God hath not promised
Skies always blue,
Flower-strewn pathways
All our lives through;
God hath not promised
Sun without rain,
Joy without sorrow,
Peace without pain.

But God hath promised
Strength for the day,
Rest for the labor,
Light for the way,
Grace for the trials,
Help from above,
Unfailing sympathy,
Undying love.

— Annie Johnson Flint

Things Are Never Quite
as Bad as They Seem

Keep up a brave spirit; things are
never quite as bad as we imagine
them to be. God always lets in the
sunshine somewhere. Hope on; no
matter how dark the way seems,
it is better farther on. Do not be
discouraged; if troubles overwhelm you,
if you have losses and crosses, or if
you are disappointed, go on hoping
and trusting; there is a good time
coming for you.

Do small things well, and you shall
be found worthy of greater ones.
Your better day will dawn!

— Author Unknown

God Never Gives Up, and Neither Should You

When you're hurt and confused
and things are hard to accept
   or understand,
give them to God
and He will give you peace and faith.

When you've been treated rudely
   or unfairly
and hatred and anger rule your soul,
talk to God about it
and He will give you a forgiving,
   calm spirit.

When you're overwhelmed with
    too much to do
and stressed out because of lack of time,
let God guide you
and He will show you where your
    priorities should be.

When you're feeling down and discouraged
and you aren't living up to your
    own dreams and expectations,
let God be your partner
and He will give you power and strength.

When things get tough and you want
    to give up,
don't...
and God won't either.

— Barbara Cage

Everything That
Touches Your Heart
Is a Gift from God

A friend who takes the time
   to stop and chat.
A smile.
A hand on your shoulder in a time of need.
An unspoken prayer
answered in a most uncommon way.
A cool breeze dancing in your hair
or a rainbow after a summer shower.
The best gift of all is to understand
that you are never alone...
because when you touch a flower,
catch that first raindrop on your fingertips,
or see the wonder of a child,
you see God.

It is the reality and profound blessing
   of knowing
that in an infinite number of ways...
God is always with you.

— Linda Hersey

In Difficult Times, Know That God Will Hold You in His Arms

It's only a matter of time before the
storms in your life subside. The clouds
will pass, and the sun will show its face.
The rain that has fallen will remind you
of the tears you've shed. There will come
a respite and a calm.

Through it all, you will feel a presence
by your side. You will sense a light
shining inside the dark corners of your
heart. That light will uplift and guide you
away from the shadows into the glorious
warmth of day.

God will hold you in His arms. He will be the rainbow at the end of your storms.

Though you may feel alone, He will hold you in His heart. He will steady your arm when you stumble. He will be your eyes when you can't see.

The storm will subside. Hope will rise to take its place, and you will break through to the light — by the grace of God.

— Josie Willis

The Power of
Daily Prayer

A breath of prayer in the morning
  Means a day of blessing sure —
A breath of prayer in the evening
  Means a night of rest secure.

A breath of prayer in our weakness
  Means the clasp of a mighty hand —
A breath of prayer when we're lonely
  Means someone to understand.

A breath of prayer in rejoicing
  Gives joy and added delight.
For they that remember God's goodness
  Go singing far into the night.

There's never a year nor a season
  That prayer may not bless every hour
And never a soul need be helpless
  When linked with God's infinite power.

— Author Unknown

With Each Sunrise,
God Gives You
a New Beginning

One of God's greatest gifts
is the chance to be
   born again each day.
Beginning with every sunrise,
you can let go of the past
and any regrets, mistakes,
   or sorrows it may have held.
You can look ahead and see
   where you'd like to go,
secure in the knowledge that
God enables you to leave
   any emotional baggage
where it belongs — in the past.
You can choose to leave
   yesterday behind
and start over again today —
to be whoever and whatever
   you dream of being.
Know that with God's help
and His constant, loving attention,
you can achieve anything...
   beginning today.

— Edmund O'Neill

The Search for God

I took a day to search for God,
And found Him not. But as I trod
   By rocky ledge, through woods untamed,
   Just where one scarlet lily flamed,
I saw His footprint in the sod.

Then suddenly, all unaware,
Far off in the deep shadows, where
   A solitary hermit thrush
   Sang through the holy twilight hush —
I heard His voice upon the air.

And even as I marveled how
God gives us Heaven here and now,
   In a stir of wind that hardly shook
   The poplar leaves beside the brook —
His hand was light upon my brow.

At last with evening as I turned
Homeward, and thought what I had learned
   And all that there was still to probe —
   I caught the glory of His robe
Where the last fires of sunset burned.

Back to the world with quickening start
I looked and longed for any part
   In making saving Beauty be...
   And from that kindling ecstasy
I knew God dwelt within my heart.

— Bliss Carman

God Is Always Listening

In your joyous moments,
He basks in your praise, thanks,
    and laughter.
When circumstances seem unjust,
    He hears your pleas.
In your times of meditative contemplation,
    He listens and inspires.
When life has dealt a low blow
And grief is your constant companion,
Your cries wrench His heart.

And in those times when you cannot speak,
Even then God hears your voice.

— Cindy B. Stevens

Let God Be Your Guide

God speaks to us through our lives,
through the smiles and the shadows,
through the times, ever changing.

God calls to us on our journeys,
    putting the broken pieces
        back together again.

God comforts us in our tears
        until life, at its worst,
            becomes something better.

God strengthens us in our weakness
        until His power is all that we feel.

God opens the door to our dreams
and gives us each day as a gift.

God feels the depth and the texture
of all our longings within.

God rejoices in our hope and our promise
as a mother rejoices over her child.

God sees only the best in the shadows
of what's yet to be.

God speaks to us through our lives,
one day and one step at a time.

— Linda E. Knight

You Will Find Peace Because...

God Has Promised
It to You

At times, you may not have peace,
and troubles may be on every side.
You may feel like giving up
because no one understands.
But a change of heart,
along with a change in thought
and adding a prayer or two,
lets God know what you're feeling.
When a prayer or even a cry
is heard from someone He loves,
He is moved with compassion.
God will be there with you
to give you comfort and strength
so that you can finish the race.
And when you cheer "I made it!",
the credit can go to Him.
Don't let the cares of life
get you down or defeat you.
Simply draw upon God's love
and stay close to Him always.
You will find peace because...
God has promised to be with you.

— Edward O'Blenis

His Light Will Inspire
Your Heart

This light can awaken dreams
It creates beauty previously unimagined
Fulfills promises and provides peace
Teaches wisdom and strengthens the weak

This light can change anything
It turns the hardest heart to tears
Transforms jealousy into gentleness
Replaces resentment with fulfillment

This light teaches forgiveness and patience
It comforts pain and soothes anger
Believes in miracles and encourages hope
Survives defeat and continues forever

This light shines on
Bright as the stars in heaven
It is a flame in the darkness of defeat
A flicker of hope that never ends
A spark to fulfill God's design for our lives

When love sparks a heart
Inspires tenderness and hope
It is always spiritual
A sign of God's light inside us

Always reach toward the light
And God will guide you from the inside
Simply follow the light
And you will find the key you need
To discover your inner beauty
And fulfill God's plan for you

— Regina Hill

God Knows...

When you are tired
and discouraged from
fruitless efforts...
God knows how hard
you have tried.
When you've cried so long
and your heart is in anguish...
God has counted your tears.
If you feel that your life
is on hold
and time has passed you by...
God is waiting with you.
When you're lonely
and your friends are too busy
even for a phone call...
God is by your side.
When you think you've tried everything
and don't know where to turn...
God has a solution.
When nothing makes sense
and you are confused
or frustrated...
God has the answer.

If suddenly your outlook is brighter
and you find traces of hope...
God has whispered to you.
When things are going well
and you have much to be
thankful for...
God has blessed you.
When something joyful happens
and you are filled with awe...
God has smiled upon you.
When you have a purpose to fulfill
and a dream to follow...
God has opened your eyes
and called you by name.
Remember that wherever you are
or whatever you're facing...
God knows.

— Kelly D. Williams

Life Can Be as Simple as a Prayer

Too often discouragement, unhappiness,
    and stress
take a toll on our lives and rob us
    of the joy we're entitled to.
It's at those times that we must not take
    the power of prayer for granted,
but we should stop what we're doing
    and focus on God.
In stressful times, we should consciously
    back off from the situation
and take a moment to reflect on what's
    really important.
A conversation with God has a way
    of putting things in perspective.
He often helps us change our attitude,
    find a solution, or see the humor.

God shows us what our talents
   and gifts are
and how to put them to use for our
   success and peace of mind.
God reminds us that mistakes and failures
   are okay;
He helps us learn from them and gives us
   the confidence to go on.
Life can be tough with all its challenges
   and problems —
we get tired and fed up, and sometimes
   we feel overwhelmed —
but it really isn't all that difficult
   when you have God...
That's when life is as simple
   as a prayer.

                       — Barbara Cage

God's Blessings
Are Ours to Cherish

There is so much to be thankful for
    in this world —
the love of our family,
a warm home, good friends,
our health and happiness,
the beauty that surrounds us.

Yet when things aren't going our way,
when sorrow enters our lives
or dreams seem out of reach,
we too quickly forget how fortunate
    we really are.

When difficulties occur,
we must learn to rise above the
feelings of sadness and despair.
We must accept the wisdom of God's plan
and go on with our lives,
grateful for His many blessings,
secure in His love.

— Anna Marie Edwards

"Please watch over someone I care about and help their sun shine through"

Oh, Lord, please watch over someone I
    care so much about. Please do it for them...
    and for me.

Please help to make this day and all that follow
    a time of comfort and understanding.
Please help the light of serenity shine in through
    an open door, warming the heart and
    encouraging the soul of somebody who
    lovingly needs to know... that they are
    dearly thought of and cared for, and that
    someone is always there for them.

Please help to chase away any clouds and
    lessen any troubles in this day.
Please help to provide the reassurance that hope,
    blessings, and a world of beautiful things are
    always there if we just take the time to see.
Please help us learn that life goes on, rainbows
    return, and the difficulties that inevitably
    come to everyone turn into insurmountable
    concerns only if we let them.

Please help us realize that problems can only
     impact us to the extent that we give
     them power over our hearts and minds.
Please empower us with patience, faith,
     and love.
Please help us choose the path we walk
     instead of letting it choose us.
Please let it take us to the brighter day that
     is always there, even though it is not
     always seen.
Please help us to be wiser than our worries,
     stronger than any situation that can
     come our way, and steadily assured
     of our beliefs.
Please help us reach the goals that wait for
     us on the horizons that encourage us.
Please enfold us within each new sunset, and
     inspire us with each new dawn.

Please help someone who is so deserving
     of every goodness and kindness life
     can bring.
          Please, Lord, help to show the way.
                              — Douglas Pagels

Anything Is Possible
Because of God

It is God who enables you
to smile in spite of tears;
to carry on when you feel like giving in;
to pray when you're at a loss for words;
to love even though your heart has been
    broken time and time again;
to sit calmly when you feel like throwing
    your hands up in frustration;
to be understanding when nothing
    seems to make sense;
to listen when you'd really rather not hear;
to share your feelings with others
    because sharing is necessary
        to ease the load.

Anything is possible
because God makes it so.

— Faye Sweeney

God Is in Control

A look around the world reminds us
that God is in control —
holding up each star,
sending sunshine down to earth,
bringing beauty into life.

One glance around the world can give
our hearts a peaceful feeling
of security in knowing that
God is watching over us.
He won't forget to let the rivers flow
or keep the flowers blooming
    in their fields.

He colors in the spaces of our lives
with moments to be thankful for
    and tender, loving care.
With His majestic touch, each night
    turns into day,
as the sun wakes up the world again
    and time blesses us once more.

It's a wondrous thing to look at life
    and realize
that the old, old story of God's love
    continues on.
He's in control and He keeps
    all things beautiful for us.

— Barbara J. Hall

May You Find Answers
to the Prayers That You Pray

May you find the gold at the end of your rainbow
May you chase every dark cloud away
May you find a way to move all your mountains
May you find answers to the prayers that you pray.

Looking back you see only what was fact,
    what was true
Looking ahead, you see your future and
    you dream of a way
As you gather up all your wishes and hide them
    in your heart
May you find answers to the prayers that you pray.

If you keep trying to reach it,
    but your goal is elusive
If you don't know whether to move on or to stay
I wish you starships to guide you and
    angels to hold you
May you find answers to the prayers that you pray.

— Donna Fargo

Let God Be Your Hope
for Every Tomorrow

God's love is like a journey
that grows more beautiful
through time.
He is your hope
for every tomorrow
and your light when
the skies are not blue.

God knows your heart
and feels your hurt;
you can trust in His strength
and lean on His caring.
His thoughts are near you
and His presence is with you;
focus on His promise
of better days ahead.

He waits by your side
with hands outstretched;
allow Him to carry
your burdens and cares.
When you have questions,
let His joy and peace
answer what you can't handle alone.
Look for God
in each part of your life,
in the love of family
and the hearts of friends.
May you live and grow
in the light of His caring,
and know that you are never alone.

— Linda E. Knight

God Is Never
Far Away

When we are hurting
God doesn't stay on high
He brings His majesty to earth
on the wings of love
When we encounter trials and tribulations
it is God who will help us face whatever
    is happening in our hearts
He pours His peace into the moments
holds our hands and calms our fears
He walks with us and talks with us
    along the way
When we need the ultimate
    in compassion —
the greatest caring, true concern —
it is God's love that wipes each tear away
and brings tomorrow's hope

God isn't far away...
    He's always by your side

— Barbara J. Hall

ACKNOWLEDGMENTS

The following is a partial list of authors whom the publisher especially wishes to thank for permission to reprint their works.

Barbara Cage for "In God, You Will Find Everything You Need," "God Never Gives Up, and Neither Should You," and "Life Can Be as Simple as a Prayer." Copyright © 2002 by Barbara Cage. All rights reserved.

Linda E. Knight for "God Will Carry You Through to New Dreams and Hopes," "Let God Be Your Guide," and "Let God Be Your Hope for Every Tomorrow." Copyright © 2002 by Linda E. Knight. All rights reserved.

Regina Hill for "Have Faith!" and "His Light Will Inspire Your Heart." Copyright © 2002 by Regina Hill. All rights reserved.

Susan Hickman Sater for "You Can Lean on Prayer for Strength and Support." Copyright © 2002 by Susan Hickman Sater. All rights reserved.

Jacqueline Schiff for "A Special Prayer for You." Copyright © 2002 by Jacqueline Schiff. All rights reserved.

Dan Lynch for "Face Your Challenges with Victory in Mind." Copyright © 2002 by Dan Lynch. All rights reserved.

PrimaDonna Entertainment Corp. for "May You Find Answers to the Prayers That You Pray" and "May These Blessings Be with You" by Donna Fargo. Copyright © 1998, 2002 by PrimaDonna Entertainment Corp. All rights reserved.

Linda Hersey for "Everything That Touches Your Heart Is a Gift from God." Copyright © 2002 by Linda Hersey. All rights reserved.

Josie Willis for "In Difficult Times, Know That God Will Hold You in His Arms." Copyright © 2002 by Josie Willis. All rights reserved.

Cindy B. Stevens for "God Is Always Listening." Copyright © 2002 by Cindy B. Stevens. All rights reserved.

Edward O'Blenis for "You Will Find Peace Because...." Copyright © 2002 by Edward O'Blenis. All rights reserved.

Barbara J. Hall for "God Is in Control." Copyright © 2002 by Barbara J. Hall. All rights reserved.

A careful effort has been made to trace the ownership of poems used in this anthology in order to obtain permission to reprint copyrighted materials and give proper credit to the copyright owners. If any error or omission has occurred, it is completely inadvertent, and we would like to make corrections in future editions provided that written notification is made to the publisher:

BLUE MOUNTAIN ARTS, Inc., P.O. Box 4549, Boulder, Colorado 80306.